The Art of Instinct: If Birds Can Be This Creative, Then Humans Can Much More!

Selasi Noamesi

Published by Selasi Noamesi, 2024.

THE ART OF INSTINCT: IF BIRDS CAN BE THIS CREATIVE, THEN HUMANS CAN MUCH MORE!

First edition. August 8, 2024.

ISBN: 979-8227277022

Written by Selasi Noamesi.

Table of Contents

THE ART OF INSTINCT ; IF BIRDS CAN BE THIS CREATIVE THEN HUMANS CAN MUCH MORE!

Introduction

In the grand tapestry of life, creativity is not a thread exclusive to humanity. Across the natural world, animals and birds exhibit remarkable ingenuity, solving complex problems, and adapting to their environments with innovative flair. From the intricate nests of weaver birds to the majestic dams of beavers, the creative genius of the natural world is on full display.

Yet, as humans, we often overlook these examples of instinctual innovation, assuming that our own creative potential is uniquely superior. But what if the boundaries between human and animal creativity were more blurred than we think? What if the instincts that drive animals to build, adapt, and thrive held secrets to unlocking our own innovative potential?

In this book, we'll embark on a journey to explore the fascinating world of animal and bird creativity, and discover how their instincts can inspire human innovation. By examining the remarkable creative feats of the natural world, we'll uncover the hidden patterns and principles that drive innovation, and learn how to tap into our own inner sources of creativity. Join me on this exploration of the art of instinct, and let's unlock the secrets of creativity that surround us.

Chapter 1

The Natural Muse

Human innovation has always been inspired by the natural world. From the intricate patterns on a butterfly's wings to the majestic strength of a tree, creation has been the ultimate muse for human creativity.

In the realm of fashion, this is particularly evident. Fabrics and clothes often incorporate elements of nature, such as floral patterns, animal prints, and textures that mimic the natural world. The beauty of a rose, the elegance of a swan, and the ferocity of a lion have all been captured in the designs of human clothing.

But it's not just fashion. Architecture, art, music, and even technology have all been influenced by the natural world. The curves of a seashell inspire the design of a skyscraper, the songs of birds influence the melodies of music, and the efficiency of a leaf's photosynthesis informs the development of solar panels.

This is because creation is not just a source of inspiration, but a testament to the ingenuity and wisdom of God. As the Psalmist writes, "The heavens declare the glory of God; the skies proclaim the work of his hands" (Psalm 19:1). In creation, we see the fingerprints of God, and it is this divine creativity that sparks our own innovation and imagination.

The Creator made the natural world full of examples of interdependence and symbiotic relationships, where different species rely on each other for survival and thrive together. This interconnectedness can inspire humans to adopt a more holistic and collaborative approach to life.

In the natural world, we see examples like:

Bees pollinating flowers, which in turn provide nectar for the bees.

Coral reefs supporting diverse marine life, which help maintain the reef's health.

Trees providing shade and shelter for animals, while animals help disperse seeds for new trees.

These relationships remind us that we are part of a larger web of life, and our actions can impact the world around us. By embracing interdependence and seeking inspiration from nature, we can:

Foster collaboration and mutual support in our communities.

Develop sustainable practices that honor the interconnectedness of our ecosystem.

Cultivate empathy and understanding for the intricate relationships within the natural world.

THE NATURAL WORLD IS a treasure trove of inspiration for human innovations and inventions. By studying the unique abilities and characteristics of animals, birds, and fish, humans have developed groundbreaking technologies and solutions.

Below are some examples of innovations inspired by animals and birds:

1. Velcro - Inspired by burrs that stick to clothing, Swiss engineer Georges de Mestral developed Velcro in the 1940s.

2. Whale Fin Wind Turbines - The curved shape of whale fins inspired more efficient wind turbine blades.

3. Sharkskin Surfaces - Researchers developed surfaces that mimic shark skin to reduce drag and prevent bacterial growth.

4. Gecko Feet Adhesives - Scientists developed adhesives inspired by geckos' ability to climb walls and ceilings.

5. Bird-Inspired Airplanes - The Wright brothers studied bird flight to develop the first successful airplane.

6. Dolphin-Inspired Sonar - Dolphins' echolocation abilities inspired the development of sonar technology.

7. Termite Mound Air Conditioning - Architects designed energy-efficient buildings inspired by termite mounds' natural ventilation systems.

8. Spider Silk Materials - Scientists developed strong, lightweight materials mimicking spider silk.

9. Fish-Inspired Submarines - Engineers designed more efficient submarines inspired by fish shapes and movements.

10. Butterfly Wing Solar Cells - Researchers developed more efficient solar cells inspired by the structure of butterfly wings.

These examples illustrate how nature has inspired human innovation, leading to groundbreaking technologies and discoveries!

HERE ARE SOME DETAILED examples of how animals and birds inspired some of these human innovations:

1. Velcro:

Georges de Mestral, a Swiss engineer, went on a hunting trip in 1941 and noticed burrs sticking to his clothing. He studied the burrs under a microscope and saw tiny hooks that caught onto loops of fabric. This inspired him to develop Velcro, a fastening system with tiny hooks and loops.

2. Whale Fin Wind Turbines:

In 2004, a team of engineers from the University of California studied the curved shape of whale fins and discovered that it increased lift and reduced drag. They applied this principle to wind turbine blades, designing a curved shape that increased energy production by 20%.

3. Sharkskin Surfaces:

Scientists studied the unique texture of shark skin, which reduces drag and prevents bacterial growth. They developed materials that mimic this texture, creating surfaces that reduce drag and prevent bacterial growth in medical devices and ships' hulls.

4. Gecko Feet Adhesives:

Researchers studied the tiny hair-like structures on geckos' feet, which create a Van der Waals force that allows them to climb walls. They developed adhesives that mimic this force, creating sticky surfaces that can hold heavy loads.

5. Bird-Inspired Airplanes:

The Wright brothers observed birds in flight and noticed that they used curved wings to generate lift. They applied this principle to their airplane design, creating a curved wing shape that enabled stable flight.

These examples illustrate how observing nature's solutions to problems led to innovative human technologies!

The intersection of nature and human innovation is a powerful space, full of possibilities and potential. By continuing to explore and learn from the natural world, we can unlock new ideas and solutions that benefit both humans and the planet!

Chapter 2

The Weaver's Wisdom

In the sun-drenched savannas of Africa, a small bird with a big reputation makes its home. The weaver bird, with its vibrant plumage and intricate nest designs, is a masterclass in creativity and innovation. These tiny architects construct elaborate nests, weaving twigs, grasses, and spider webs into sturdy yet elegant structures that cradle their young. The weaver bird's creativity is not just about aesthetics; it's a matter of survival. Their nests must withstand fierce storms, predators, and rival birds. To achieve this, they employ a range of innovative techniques:

Experimentation: Weaver birds try out different materials and designs, adapting to what works best.

Problem-solving: They overcome obstacles like wind, rain, and predators with clever solutions.

Attention to detail: Each nest is meticulously crafted, with precise placement of every twig and thread.

As we observe the weaver bird's creative process, we begin to see parallels with human innovation:

Embracing failure: Weaver birds don't give up when their nests fail; they learn and try again.

Collaboration: Some species of weaver birds work together to build complex nests.

Adaptation: They adjust their designs to suit changing environments and needs.

The weaver bird's wisdom offers valuable lessons for human creatives:

Don't be afraid to experiment and try new approaches.

Pay attention to details, but also see the bigger picture.

Collaborate and learn from others.

As we delve deeper into the natural world, we'll discover more examples of animal and bird creativity that can inspire human innovation. The weaver bird's nests embody the power of instinctual creativity.

The weaver bird's remarkable abilities despite its physical limitations are a testament to the incredible potential that lies within every living being.

If a small bird without hands can achieve such remarkable feats, imagine what humans can accomplish with our:

1. Larger brain capacity

2. Advanced cognitive abilities

3. Dexterity and fine motor skills

4. Capacity for complex problem-solving

5. Ability to learn from experience and adapt

The weaver bird's example encourages us to push beyond our perceived limitations and tap into our inner potential. We can learn to:

1. Be more resourceful and creative

2. Develop innovative solutions to complex problems

3. Collaborate and work together towards common goals

4. Adapt to changing circumstances and environments

5. Achieve extraordinary things despite our own limitations

By embracing the weaver bird's spirit of ingenuity and determination, we can unlock our own potential and achieve remarkable things!

THE ENGINEER'S EYE

In the heart of North America's wilderness, a remarkable engineer is hard at work. The beaver, with its flat tail and industrious nature, is a master builder, constructing dams and lodges that transform its environment. These incredible structures are testaments to the beaver's innovative spirit and creativity. Beavers are ecosystem engineers, shaping their surroundings to suit their needs. Their dams:

Control water flow: Creating ponds, wetlands, and habitats for countless species.

Provide protection: Safeguarding against predators and harsh weather.

Enable community: Supporting complex social structures and family life.

The beaver's creative approach offers valuable insights for human innovators:

Systems thinking: Beavers consider the broader ecosystem when building their dams.

Resourcefulness: They repurpose materials, using trees, mud, and rocks to construct their creations.

Resilience: Beavers adapt and maintain their dams, ensuring their survival.

As we examine the beaver's remarkable engineering feats, we can learn to:

Think holistically, considering the wider impact of our creations.

Embrace resourcefulness, finding innovative solutions with available materials.

Cultivate resilience, adapting and maintaining our creations in the face of challenges.

The beaver's remarkable abilities remind us that creativity is not limited to artistic expression; it can also be found in the problem-solving, innovative spirit of engineers and builders. By embracing the beaver's engineer's eye, we can unlock new potential for creative solutions in our own lives.

THE ARTISAN'S TOUCH

In the lush rainforests of Australia, a tiny king of creativity reigns supreme. The bowerbird, with its vibrant plumage and exquisite courtship displays, is a master artisan, crafting intricate structures that showcase its beauty and charm. Male bowerbirds construct elaborate bowers, adorned with:

Colorful trinkets: Shells, berries, and feathers, carefully arranged to impress potential mates.

Intricate architecture: Delicate twig and leaf structures, showcasing the bird's skill and patience.

Personalized decor: Unique arrangements, reflecting the individual bird's style and creativity.

The bowerbird's artisanal approach offers valuable lessons for human creatives:

Attention to detail: Bowerbirds meticulously arrange each element, demonstrating the power of precision.

Personal expression: Each bower reflects the individual bird's character, highlighting the importance of authenticity.

Storytelling: Bowerbirds use their creations to communicate and connect with others, illustrating the impact of narrative.

As we marvel at the bowerbird's artistic achievements, we can learn to:

THE ART OF INSTINCT: IF BIRDS CAN BE THIS CREATIVE, THEN HUMANS CAN MUCH MORE!

Hone our attention to detail, refining our craft and creativity.

Embrace our unique voice, celebrating individuality in our work.

Weave storytelling into our creations, connecting with others on a deeper level.

The bowerbird's remarkable artistry reminds us that creativity can be found in the intricate, the delicate, and the beautiful. By embracing the artisan's touch, we can unlock new possibilities for innovation and self-expression.

Chapter 3

Biblical Exploration

LET'S NOW EXPLORE SOME biblical examples of our discourse:

PROVERBS 6:6-8 (NIV)

"Go to the ant, you sluggard; consider its ways and be wise! It has no commander, no overseer or ruler, yet it stores its provisions in summer and gathers its food at harvest. How long will you lie there, you sluggard? When will you get up from your sleep?"

Inspiration from Ants:

Industry and Hard Work: Ants are incredibly diligent and hardworking creatures. They labor tirelessly to gather food and store provisions, even though they have no centralized authority or ruler.

Self-Motivation and Initiative: Ants don't need external motivation or supervision to work hard. They're self-driven and take initiative to achieve their goals.

Planning and Preparation: Ants plan ahead, storing food during summer for the leaner winter months. They're prepared for the future and don't procrastinate.

They're predictive creatures.

Teamwork and Collaboration: Ants work together to achieve common goals, often in complex social hierarchies.

Application to Human Creativity and Innovation:

Emulate the ant's industry and hard work in your creative pursuits. Be diligent and persistent in your efforts.

Take self-motivated initiative to drive your projects forward, even when faced with challenges or uncertainty.

Plan and prepare for the future, anticipating potential obstacles and opportunities.

Collaborate with others, leveraging diverse skills and strengths to achieve common goals.

By embracing these principles, we can tap into the wisdom of ants and enhance our own creativity, innovation, and productivity.

If tiny ants, with their limited size and resources, can demonstrate such wisdom and ingenuity, then the potential within us is vast and untapped.

Just as ants work together, plan, and persevere, we too can harness our collective strengths, creativity, and determination to achieve greatness.

By embracing these qualities and recognizing our own unique abilities, we can unlock our full potential and make a meaningful impact in the world.

Remember, it's not about being the biggest or the strongest; it's about being wise, working together, and striving for excellence. So, let's tap into our inner "ant wisdom" and unleash our full potential!

AGAIN, JOB 38:36 (KJV) says: "Who hath put wisdom in the inward parts? or who hath given understanding to the heart?" This verse suggests that God has instilled wisdom and understanding within the hearts and minds of all creatures, including animals. It implies that every living being has a unique form of wisdom and intuition that enables them to navigate their environments and make decisions.

In the context of creativity and innovation, this verse encourages us to:

1. Recognize the inherent wisdom in all creatures: Acknowledge that every living being has a unique perspective and wisdom to offer.

2. Learn from nature and its inhabitants: Observe and learn from the behaviors, adaptations, and problem-solving strategies of animals and other creatures.

3. Tap into the collective wisdom of creation: Draw inspiration and insight from the natural world and its inhabitants to inform our creative pursuits and innovations.

This perspective can inspire us to cultivate a deeper appreciation for the wisdom and creativity present in all living beings and harness that collective wisdom to drive innovation and progress.

THE HAWK AND EAGLE

We can also see Job 39:26-30 (KJV)

"Doth the hawk fly by thy wisdom, and stretch her wings toward the south?

Doth the eagle mount up at thy command, and make her nest on high?

She dwelleth and abideth on the rock, upon the crag of the rock, and the strong place.

From thence she seeketh the prey, and her eyes behold afar off.

Her young ones also suck up blood: and where the slain are, there is she."

The above passage also reveals the incredible abilities and instincts of birds, specifically the hawk and eagle. It emphasizes that their remarkable behaviors and skills are not solely the result of human wisdom or command, but rather an innate wisdom and guidance from God. This passage encourages us to:

1. Marvel at the natural world's complexity and beauty: Recognize the awe-inspiring abilities and instincts of creatures like the hawk and eagle among others.

2. Acknowledge the limitations of human wisdom: Understand that there are aspects of creation that operate independently of human knowledge or control.

3. Seek inspiration from nature's designs and patterns: Observe and learn from the remarkable adaptations and strategies of birds and other creatures to inform our own creative pursuits and innovations.

4. Trust in God's sovereignty and guidance: Recognize that God's wisdom and guidance extend to all creation, and trust in His providence and care.

In the context of creativity and innovation, this passage inspires us to:

Emulate the hawk's and eagle's remarkable abilities, such as their keen eyesight, adaptability, and resilience.

Develop innovative solutions that mirror the natural world's efficiency and effectiveness.

Trust in God's guidance and wisdom as we navigate the creative process.

By these principles, we can tap into the wisdom and creativity present in the natural world and reflect God's glory through our innovative endeavors.

If the above birds, with their remarkable abilities and instincts, demonstrate such wisdom and guidance from God, then humans have even greater potential for wisdom, creativity, and innovation.

THE ART OF INSTINCT: IF BIRDS CAN BE THIS CREATIVE, THEN HUMANS CAN MUCH MORE!

As created beings, humans possess a unique capacity for complex thought, problem-solving, and innovation. By acknowledging and embracing the wisdom and guidance from God, humans can tap into their full potential and achieve remarkable things.

Just as birds soar to great heights and navigate with precision, humans can:

Soar to new heights of creativity and innovation.

Navigate complex challenges with wisdom and discernment.

Build strong foundations for their lives and communities.

Seek out new horizons and opportunities

Nurture and empower future generations.

WISE AS SERPENTS

Jesus said: "Behold, I send you forth as sheep in the midst of wolves: be ye therefore wise as serpents, and harmless as doves." - Matthew 10:16 (KJV)

This verse encourages us to:

1. Emulate the serpent's wisdom: Serpents are known for their cunning, adaptability, and strategic thinking. Jesus advises us to adopt these qualities in our interactions and decision-making.

2. Balance wisdom with innocence: While being wise as serpents, we should also maintain the harmless and gentle nature

of doves. This balance ensures that our wisdom is used for good and not exploited for personal gain or harm.

In the context of creativity and innovation, being "wise as serpents" means:

Embracing adaptability and resilience in the face of challenges.

Employing strategic thinking and creative problem-solving.

Navigating complex situations with discernment and intuition.

Balancing wisdom with humility and a willingness to learn.

Let's dive deeper into the wisdom of the serpent:

Cunning and adaptability: Serpents are known for their ability to navigate complex environments and adapt to new situations. We can learn from their flexibility and resourcefulness.

Strategic thinking: Serpents are calculated in their movements and decisions. We can emulate their strategic approach to problem-solving and planning.

Stealth and subtlety: Serpents often achieve their goals without drawing attention to themselves. We can learn from their subtlety and ability to work behind the scenes.

Resilience and persistence: Serpents are notorious for their ability to survive and thrive in challenging environments. We can adopt their determination and perseverance.

In the context of creativity and innovation, embracing the wisdom of the serpent means:

Embracing flexibility and adaptability in our creative processes.

Employing strategic thinking to navigate complex problems and opportunities.

Working subtly and collaboratively to achieve our goals.

Persisting through challenges and setbacks with determination and resilience.

As we embrace the wisdom of the serpent, we can develop innovative solutions that are both effective and wise, reflecting the teachings of Jesus and the natural world. By embracing this wisdom, we can develop innovative solutions that are both effective and ethical, reflecting Jesus' teachings and values.

FOUR WISE CREATURES

Proverbs 30:24-28 (KJV)

"There be four things which are little upon the earth, but they are exceeding wise: The ants are a people not strong, yet they prepare their meat in the summer; The conies are but a feeble folk, yet make they their houses in the rocks; The locusts have no king, yet go they forth all of them by bands; The spider taketh hold with her hands, and is in kings' palaces."

This passage reveals the wisdom of four small creatures:

1. Ants: As we've seen, despite their weakness, ants prepare for the future by storing food during summer.

2. Conies (or hyraxes): Although feeble, conies build secure homes in rocky crevices.

3. Locusts: Without a king, locusts march together in organized bands.

4. Spiders: With their delicate hands, spiders infiltrate even royal palaces.

This passage teaches us to:

1. Prepare for the future like ants, who store food for lean times.

2. Build secure foundations like conies, who construct safe homes.

3. Collaborate and organize like locusts, who work together without a leader.

4. Be resourceful and opportunistic like spiders, who thrive in unexpected places.

In the context of creativity and innovation, this passage inspires us to:

1. Plan and prepare for our creative endeavors.

2. Build strong foundations for our ideas and projects.

3. Collaborate and work together with others towards common goals.

4. Seize opportunities and adapt to new situations like the resourceful spider.

THE ART OF INSTINCT: IF BIRDS CAN BE THIS CREATIVE, THEN HUMANS CAN MUCH MORE!

By exploring the wisdom of these small creatures, we can develop innovative solutions and achieve greatness despite our limitations.

Chapter 4

The Roots of Innovation

As we explore the fascinating world of animal and bird creativity, it's essential to understand the evolutionary roots of innovation. Why do certain species develop remarkable creative abilities, while others do not? What drives the emergence of innovative traits, and how can we apply these insights to human creativity? In this chapter, we'll delve into the evolutionary pressures and mechanisms that shape creative abilities in the natural world. We'll examine:

Adaptation and survival: How creative traits enhance survival and reproductive success.

Neurobiological foundations: The brain structures and processes that underlie creative abilities.

Social and environmental factors: How social interaction, culture, and environment influence innovation.

By understanding the evolutionary roots of innovation, we can:

Identify key drivers of creativity: Recognizing the factors that spark innovative traits.

Foster creative environments: Encouraging social and environmental conditions that support innovation.

THE ART OF INSTINCT: IF BIRDS CAN BE THIS CREATIVE, THEN HUMANS CAN MUCH MORE!

Unlock human potential: Applying evolutionary insights to enhance our own creative abilities.

The evolutionary perspective offers a unique lens through which to view creativity, highlighting the dynamic interplay between species, environment, and innovation. By exploring the roots of innovation, we can gain a deeper appreciation for the creative forces that shape our world.

Adaptation and Survival

In the natural world, creativity is often a matter of life and death. Species that develop innovative traits are more likely to survive and reproduce, passing those traits on to their offspring. Let's look at some examples:

Crows, renowned for their intelligence, use sticks to retrieve food from hard-to-reach places. This creative tool use allows them to access resources that other birds can't, giving them a survival advantage.

Chimpanzees use rocks to crack open nuts, demonstrating problem-solving skills that help them thrive in their environment.

Octopuses change color to camouflage themselves, showcasing adaptability and creativity in the face of predators.

These examples illustrate how creative traits can enhance survival and reproductive success. By understanding how species adapt and innovate, we can apply those lessons to human creativity.

Neurobiological Foundations

What happens in the brain when we're creative? Let's explore the neurobiological foundations of innovation:

Neuroplasticity and adaptability allow our brains to reorganize and refine connections, enabling creative thinking.

Dopamine and reward systems drive us to explore and experiment, fueling innovation.

Default mode networks and mind-wandering enable us to make novel connections and generate new ideas.

By understanding the neural basis of creativity, we can unlock new strategies for enhancing our own innovative potential.

Social and Environmental Factors

Creativity is often shaped by our social and environmental context. Let's examine how these factors influence innovation:

Social learning and cultural transmission allow us to learn from others and build upon existing knowledge.

Environmental pressures and constraints can stimulate creative problem-solving.

Group dynamics and collaboration can foster innovative thinking and idea generation.

Examples include:

Birds learning songs from each other, showcasing social learning and cultural transmission.

Primates adopting new tools through social interaction, highlighting the role of group dynamics.

Termites building complex societies with division of labor, demonstrating the power of collaboration.

When we recognize the interplay between social, environmental, and creative factors, we can design environments that foster innovation and enhance our own creative potential.

Unlocking Human Potential

By understanding the evolutionary roots of innovation, we can unlock new insights and strategies for enhancing human creativity. Here are some takeaways:

Embrace experimentation and risk-taking, just like crows and chimpanzees.

Cultivate neuroplasticity through learning and practice, allowing your brain to adapt and refine connections.

Leverage social learning and cultural transmission by collaborating with others and building upon existing knowledge.

Use environmental pressures and constraints as stimuli for creative problem-solving.

Foster group dynamics and collaboration to generate innovative ideas.

By applying these lessons from the natural world, we can:

Enhance our own creative potential.

Design environments that foster innovation.

Develop novel solutions to complex problems.

Case Study: Biomimicry

Biomimicry, the practice of emulating nature to solve human problems, as we've seen, is a powerful example of how understanding evolutionary innovation can drive human creativity. By studying nature's solutions to complex challenges, we can develop novel technologies and innovative solutions. Examples of biomimicry include:

Velcro, inspired by burrs that stick to clothing.

Whale fin wind turbines, mimicking the efficient shape of whale fins.

Gecko-inspired adhesives, replicating the sticky properties of gecko feet.

Chapter 5

From Instinct to Innovation

As we've explored the fascinating world of animal and bird creativity, it's clear that instinct plays a vital role in their innovative abilities. But how can humans tap into our own instincts to spark innovation? In this chapter, we'll delve into the relationship between instinct and innovation, exploring:

The Power of Subconscious Thinking: How our subconscious mind can drive creative insights and innovative solutions.

Embracing Intuition: Trusting our instincts to guide us toward novel ideas and approaches.

Cultivating Mindfulness: Staying present and aware to tap into our instinctual creative potential.

By understanding the interplay between instinct and innovation, we can:

Unlock New Sources of Creativity: Tapping into our subconscious mind and intuition to generate novel ideas.

Enhance Our Problem-Solving Abilities: Using instinct to navigate complex challenges and find innovative solutions.

Foster a Culture of Creativity: Encouraging others to embrace their instincts and intuition, driving collective innovation.

THE ART OF INSTINCT: IF BIRDS CAN BE THIS CREATIVE, THEN HUMANS CAN MUCH MORE!

Let's explore how humans can harness the power of instinct to drive innovation, and what lessons we can learn from the natural world to spark our own creative potential.

THE POWER OF SUBCONSCIOUS Thinking

Our subconscious mind plays a vital role in creative problem-solving and innovation. By tapping into our subconscious, we can access novel ideas and insights that might elude us through conscious thinking alone. Let's explore how to harness the power of subconscious thinking:

Incubation: Allow yourself time to relax and disengage from a problem, letting your subconscious work on it in the background.

Mind-wandering: Engage in activities that let your mind wander, like walking or meditation, to tap into subconscious thoughts.

Dreaming: Pay attention to your dreams, as they can reveal hidden connections and innovative ideas.

Embracing Intuition

Intuition is a powerful driver of creativity and innovation. By trusting our instincts, we can navigate complex challenges and find novel solutions. Let's examine how to embrace intuition:

Listen to your gut: Pay attention to your initial reactions and instincts, even if they seem illogical.

Trust your instincts: Have confidence in your ability to make decisions and navigate uncertainty.

Practice self-awareness: Understand your own thought patterns and biases to better trust your intuition.

Cultivating Mindfulness

Mindfulness is essential for tapping into our instinctual creative potential. By staying present and aware, we can access novel ideas and insights. Let's explore mindfulness practices:

Meditation: Regular meditation practice can help quiet the mind and access subconscious thoughts.

Presence: Focus on the present moment, letting go of distractions and mental clutter.

Awareness: Cultivate self-awareness to recognize your thoughts, emotions, and instincts.

The power of subconscious thinking, intuition, and mindfulness, can help unlock new sources of creativity and innovation. Remember, instinct is a powerful driver of creative potential – trust it, and let it guide you toward novel ideas and solutions.

INSTINCTUAL INNOVATION in Action

Let's explore some real-world examples of instinctual innovation in action:

Steve Jobs and Apple: Jobs' intuition and instinctual design sense revolutionized the tech industry.

Albert Einstein and Relativity: Einstein's thought experiments and intuition led to groundbreaking scientific discoveries.

These examples among others demonstrate how instinct can drive innovation and creativity. By embracing our own instincts, we can:

Make novel connections: Combine seemingly unrelated ideas to create something new.

Navigate uncertainty: Trust our instincts to guide us through complex challenges.

Create innovative solutions: Tap into our subconscious mind to find novel answers.

INSTINCTUAL INNOVATION in Teams

Instinctual innovation can also be applied to teams and organizations. By fostering a culture of instinctual creativity, teams can:

Encourage wild ideas: Create a safe space for sharing novel and unconventional ideas.

Trust collective instincts: Leverage the collective intuition of team members to make decisions.

Embrace experimentation: Encourage experimentation and learning from failure.

THE HUMAN BRAIN HAS a vast and impressive capacity for:

1. Storage: Estimated to be around 100 terabytes (TB) of information, comparable to the storage capacity of about 20 million hours of music or 400,000 hours of movies.

2. Processing: Capable of processing 1 exaflop (1 billion billion calculations) per second, making it one of the most powerful processors known.

3. Neurons: Contains approximately 86 billion neurons, each capable of forming thousands of connections with other neurons.

4. Synapses: Estimated to have around 100 trillion synapses, which facilitate communication between neurons.

5. Memory: Can store up to 100,000 terabytes of information in long-term memory, with some estimates suggesting even higher capacities.

6. Learning: Capable of reorganizing and adapting throughout life in response to new experiences and learning.

7. Creativity: Enables humans to generate new ideas, solutions, and innovations.

8. Emotions: Processes and regulates emotions, influencing behavior, decision-making, and relationships.

9. Language: Facilitates complex language processing, understanding, and generation.

10. Consciousness: Supports awareness, self-awareness, and the human experience.

These capacities make the human brain a remarkable and intricate organ, essential for our existence and potential.

Chapter 6

Flocking to Innovation

In the natural world, flocking behavior is a powerful driver of innovation. By studying how birds and other animals flock together, we can learn valuable lessons about collaboration, adaptability, and creative problem-solving. In this chapter, we'll explore:

The Science of Flocking: How animals use collective behavior to achieve remarkable feats.

Flocking in Human Teams: How to apply flocking principles to human collaboration and innovation.

Adaptability and Resilience: How flocking behavior can help teams adapt to changing environments and challenges.

By embracing the principles of flocking, we can:

Enhance collaboration and communication.

Drive collective creativity and innovation.

Build resilient and adaptable teams.

Let's dive into the fascinating world of flocking behavior and discover how it can inspire human innovation.

The Science of Flocking

THE ART OF INSTINCT: IF BIRDS CAN BE THIS CREATIVE, THEN HUMANS CAN MUCH MORE!

Flocking behavior is a remarkable phenomenon in the natural world, where individual animals follow simple rules to create complex patterns and achieve remarkable feats. By studying flocking behavior, we can gain insights into:

Self-organization: How individual animals follow local rules to create global patterns.

Decentralized decision-making: How flocking behavior emerges without centralized control.

Adaptability and resilience: How flocks respond to changing environments and predators.

Examples of flocking behavior include:

Birds flying in formation: Creating aerodynamic benefits and confusing predators.

Schools of fish: Evading predators and finding food through collective behavior.

Ant colonies: Building complex underground societies through decentralized decision-making.

FLOCKING IN HUMAN TEAMS

By applying flocking principles to human collaboration, we can:

Enhance communication and coordination.

Drive collective creativity and innovation.

Build adaptable and resilient teams.

Strategies for flocking in human teams include:

Decentralized decision-making: Empowering individuals to make local decisions.

Simple rules and guidelines: Establishing clear expectations and protocols.

Adaptive leadership: Encouraging experimentation and learning from failure.

Adaptability and Resilience

Flocking behavior can help teams adapt to changing environments and challenges by:

Embracing uncertainty and ambiguity.

Encouraging experimentation and learning.

Fostering a culture of resilience and adaptability.

Chapter 7

Migration and Movement

In the natural world, migration and movement are essential for survival and innovation. As animals and birds migrate, they navigate uncharted territories, adapt to new environments, and discover new resources. Similarly, human teams can apply the principles of migration to drive innovation and growth. By embracing change and uncertainty, we can cultivate a mindset of adaptability and resilience, leading to groundbreaking discoveries and success.

In this chapter, we'll delve into:

The Science of Migration: How animals navigate and adapt during migration

Movement and Innovation: How human teams can apply migration principles to drive innovation

Embracing Change and Uncertainty: How to cultivate a mindset of adaptability and resilience

By embracing the principles of migration and movement, we can:

Navigate complex challenges and uncertainty

Drive innovation and growth

Cultivate adaptability and resilience

Let's explore the fascinating world of migration and movement, and discover how it can inspire human innovation.

The Science of Migration

Migration is an incredible feat of navigation, adaptation, and resilience. By studying how animals migrate, we can gain insights into:

Genetic predisposition: How some animals are born with innate migration routes and schedules

Environmental cues: How animals use environmental signals like daylight, temperature, and food availability to navigate.

Social learning: How animals learn migration routes and strategies from each other.

Examples of remarkable migrations include:

Monarch butterflies: Traveling thousands of miles from Canada to Mexico each year.

Humpback whales: Migrating up to 16,000 miles annually from polar to tropical waters.

Arctic terns: Flying up to 44,000 miles each year from the Arctic to the Antarctic

Movement and Innovation

By applying migration principles to human teams, we can:

Drive innovation and growth.

Cultivate adaptability and resilience.

Navigate complex challenges and uncertainty.

Strategies for movement and innovation include:

Embracing change and uncertainty.

Exploring new environments and contexts.

Finding new resources and opportunities.

Embracing Change and Uncertainty

To cultivate a mindset of adaptability and resilience, we can:

Practice flexibility and openness.

Encourage experimentation and learning.

Foster a culture of adaptability and resilience.

Case Study: Migration and Innovation in Business

Companies like Airbnb and Uber have successfully applied migration principles to drive innovation and growth. By embracing change and uncertainty, they have:

Identified new markets and opportunities.

Adapted to changing customer needs and preferences.

Navigated complex regulatory environments.

The Art of Navigation

Migration and movement require incredible navigation skills. By studying how animals navigate, we can learn valuable lessons about:

Reading environmental cues.

Using mental maps and spatial memory.

Adapting to changing circumstances.

These navigation skills can be applied to human teams to:

Make better decisions.

Navigate complex challenges.

Drive innovation and growth.

The Power of Restlessness

Migration and movement are driven by a sense of restlessness and discontent. By embracing this restlessness, we can:

Challenge assumptions and status quo.

Explore new possibilities and opportunities.

Drive innovation and growth.

Let's continue to explore the fascinating world of migration and movement, and discover how it can inspire human innovation.

Embracing Restlessness in Teams

To cultivate a sense of restlessness in teams, leaders can:

Encourage experimentation and learning.

Foster a culture of curiosity and inquiry.

Embrace failure as an opportunity for growth.

By embracing restlessness, teams can:

Stay adaptable and resilient.

Drive innovation and growth.

Navigate complex challenges and uncertainty.

THE ART OF STOPOVER

THE ART OF INSTINCT: IF BIRDS CAN BE THIS CREATIVE, THEN HUMANS CAN MUCH MORE!

During migration, animals often make stopovers to rest and refuel. By studying these stopovers, we can learn valuable lessons about:

The importance of rest and relaxation

The need for refueling and rejuvenation

The value of community and social connection

These lessons can be applied to human teams to:

Improve productivity and performance

Enhance well-being and job satisfaction

Foster a sense of community and collaboration

The Power of Return

Migration and movement often involve a return journey. By studying these return journeys, we can learn valuable lessons about:

The importance of reflection and evaluation

The need for closure and completion

The value of sharing knowledge and experience

These lessons can be applied to human teams to:

Improve learning and development

Enhance innovation and growth

Foster a sense of shared purpose and direction.

Chapter 8

Hibernation and Dormancy

In the natural world, hibernation and dormancy are essential strategies for survival and renewal. By studying how animals and birds hibernate and enter dormant states, we can learn valuable lessons about:

Conservation of energy and resources

Protection from harsh environments and predators

Renewal and rejuvenation

In this chapter, we'll explore:

The Science of Hibernation: How animals prepare for and enter hibernation

Dormancy in Human Teams: How to apply hibernation principles to drive innovation and growth

Renewal and Rejuvenation: How to cultivate a culture of rest and relaxation

By embracing the principles of hibernation and dormancy, we can:

Conserve energy and resources

Protect ourselves from burnout and exhaustion

Renew and rejuvenate ourselves for innovation and growth

Let's dive into the fascinating world of hibernation and dormancy, and discover how it can inspire human innovation.

The Science of Hibernation

Hibernation is a state of inactivity and reduced metabolism that some animals enter to conserve energy and survive harsh environments. By studying hibernation, we can learn about:

Preparation and anticipation: How animals prepare for hibernation by storing food and slowing down their metabolism

Physiological changes: How animals' bodies change during hibernation, such as reduced heart rate and body temperature

Arousal and emergence: How animals wake up from hibernation and return to normal activity

Examples of hibernating animals include:

Bears: Hibernating for months during winter to conserve energy.

Bats: Hibernating during winter to survive cold temperatures.

Marmots: Hibernating for up to 8 months to conserve energy and survive harsh alpine environments.

Dormancy in Human Teams

By applying hibernation principles to human teams, we can:

Conserve energy and resources

Protect ourselves from burnout and exhaustion

Renew and rejuvenate ourselves for innovation and growth.

Strategies for dormancy in human teams include:

Taking breaks and time off.

Prioritizing self-care and relaxation.

Fostering a culture of rest and rejuvenation.

Renewal and Rejuvenation.

By cultivating a culture of rest and relaxation, we can:

Improve productivity and performance.

Enhance creativity and innovation.

Build resilience and adaptability.

Chapter 9

The Human Edge

Introduction

In the previous chapters, we explored the fascinating world of animal instinct and creativity. We saw how animals adapt, innovate, and thrive in their environments. But what about humans? What sets us apart from the animal kingdom? In this chapter, we'll delve into the unique aspects of human creativity and explore what makes us distinct.

Imagination and Abstract Thinking

Humans possess a remarkable ability to imagine and think abstractly. We can conceptualize ideas, envision possibilities, and create mental scenarios. This capacity for imagination allows us to:

Envision and create new futures

Develop complex theories and models

Craft stories and art that inspire and connect us

Emotional Intelligence and Empathy

Humans are wired to connect with others on a deep emotional level. We can empathize, understand, and relate to others' experiences. This emotional intelligence enables us to:

Build strong relationships and communities

Communicate effectively and resolve conflicts

THE ART OF INSTINCT: IF BIRDS CAN BE THIS CREATIVE, THEN HUMANS CAN MUCH MORE!

Create art and stories that resonate with others

Capacity for Complex Problem-Solving

Humans have an incredible ability to tackle complex problems and find innovative solutions. We can:

Analyze complex systems and identify patterns.

Develop and apply new technologies.

Collaborate and share knowledge to drive progress.

Ability to Learn from Experience and Adapt

Humans have a remarkable capacity to learn from experience, adapt to new situations, and evolve over time. We can:

Reflect on our experiences and adjust our approaches.

Learn from failures and successes.

Develop new skills and expertise.

These unique aspects of human creativity – imagination, emotional intelligence, complex problem-solving, and adaptability – form the foundation of our innovative potential.

The Power of Human Creativity

When we combine our imagination, emotional intelligence, complex problem-solving, and adaptability, we unlock the full potential of human creativity. We can:

Envision and create new possibilities.

Develop innovative solutions to complex challenges.

Craft meaningful connections and relationships.

Drive progress and evolution.

The Human Edge in Action

We see the human edge in action in various fields, such as:

Art and design, where imagination and creativity shine

Science and technology, where complex problem-solving and adaptability drive innovation

Social impact and community building, where emotional intelligence and empathy make a difference

Conclusion

In this chapter, we explored the unique aspects of human creativity and what sets us apart from the animal kingdom. By embracing our imagination, emotional intelligence, complex problem-solving, and adaptability, we can unlock our full potential and drive innovation, progress, and positive change.

Chapter 10

Collaborating with Nature

Introduction

In the previous chapters, we explored the fascinating world of animal instinct and creativity, the unique aspects of human creativity, and how to apply animal-inspired creativity to drive human innovation. Now, let's delve into the potential for human-animal co-creativity and collaboration.

Collaborative Problem-Solving with Animals

By working with animals, we can:

Leverage their unique skills and abilities.

Gain new insights and perspectives.

Develop more effective solutions to complex challenges.

Using Animal Intelligence to Inform Human Design

Animals can inform human design and innovation through:

Biomimicry and biologically-inspired design.

Animal-centered design and user experience.

Co-creation and participatory design with animals.

Exploring the Ethical Implications of Human-Animal Collaboration

As we collaborate with animals, we must consider:

Animal welfare and well-being.

Consent and agency in animal participation.

Power dynamics and fairness in human-animal collaboration.

Case Studies and Examples

Some remarkable examples of human-animal collaboration, include:

Animal-assisted therapy and healthcare.

Conservation efforts and wildlife preservation.

Service animals and assistive technologies.

By the knowledge of the human-animal co-creativity, we can drive innovation, sustainability, and positive change.

Conclusion

In this chapter, we explored the potential for human-animal collaboration and co-creativity. By working with animals and leveraging their unique skills and abilities, we can develop more effective solutions to complex challenges and drive positive change.

Conclusion of the book

As we conclude our journey through the fascinating world of animal instinct and creativity, and the exploration of human creativity and innovation, let's summarize the key takeaways:

Animals possess remarkable creativity and problem-solving abilities that can inspire human innovation.

Humans have unique creative strengths, including imagination, emotional intelligence, complex problem-solving, and adaptability.

By embracing animal-inspired creativity and collaborating with nature, we can drive innovation, sustainability, and positive change.

Now, we encourage you to embrace your own creative potential:

Explore the natural world and let animal instinct inspire your creativity.

Cultivate your unique human strengths and abilities.

Collaborate with others, including animals, to drive innovation and progress.

Remember, creativity is a powerful force that can transform individuals, communities, and the world. By embracing our creative potential and working together, we can create a brighter, more sustainable future for all.

Embracing the Creative Spark Within

As you close this book, we hope you've discovered the creative spark within yourself. Fan that spark into a flame, and let it guide you on your own journey of innovation and discovery. Together, let's unleash a wave of creativity that can change the world. Thank you for joining me on this journey!

ABOUT THE AUTHOR

Selasi Evans Noamesi is an anointed man of God who operates in the dynamics of God's power, in healing, miracles and the prophetic. He is a dynamic teacher of the Word of God, bringing fresh insights and revelations from the heart of God in the Bible, through the lens of the Cross of Christ, to the Body of Christ. He is the founder of the Eternal Assembly of Christ, a ministry currently in Ghana, West Africa.

He is a prolific writer who has PhD in Theology.

Contact Information: call/WhatsApp +233241227470/ +233204897476

Facebook: Apostle Selasi E.N Epiphanes / Selasi Evans Noamesi

www.ingramcontent.com/pod-product-compliance
Lightning Source LLC
La Vergne TN
LVHW040918150826
845672LV00007B/2096

9798227277022